tap dancing in my socks

Bill Kenney

tap dancing in my socks

copyright © 2022 Bill Kenney
ISBN 978-1-958408-09-4

Red Moon Press
PO Box 2461
Winchester VA
22604-1661 USA
www.redmoonpress.com

first printing

to my friends

KAREN BENNETT

and

JOCELYN CAMP

for being there

tap dancing

in my socks

between

getting older
the people
I call old

we called it ugly
when it was new —
vintage car

swift running brook
the line between
theirs and ours

moving in the echoes we make

my neighbor's cat
surveys the parking lot
I need a new car

bonsai
she straightens
my tie

staff meeting
straightening
a paper clip

a pain I haven't
mentioned to the doctor
summer's end

long sermon
on the Holy Trinity —
my divided attention

graveside
the sun
on my back

old photo
her face before
she knew mine

getting older
the people
I call young

snap

departing spring
she waits for me
to catch up

cold snap
a bite
of the radish

rainy autumn . . .
the last time we did it
a second time

departing geese
my promise
to a child

rain at dawn
tap dancing
in my socks

dawn woods
ankle-deep
in autumn

autumn rain
the weight of
my eyelids

happy hour
we don't mention
the cancer

chemo . . .
midtown traffic
stop and go

deep winter
the new neighbor
has cleared my path

stop buzzing, fly —
there's nothing out there
but winter

last call
the bartender takes off
his Santa hat

somewhere

cleared for takeoff
the flight attendant adjusts
her bra strap

cruising . . .
cloud shadows cling
to the earth

mountain lake
sunrise
all the way down

hitchhiker
in the rearview mirror
big sky

mountain sunrise
the rattle of a truck
headed somewhere else

small town diner
the waitress asks me
where I'm headed

heavy traffic
yesterday's mountain
somewhere in the mist

crow on a branch
staring at the Pacific
our silence

jacaranda
from here to the corner
I step lightly

sugar

rom-com
sharing the armrest
with a stranger

safe sex
saying nothing
I'll regret

original sin —
trying to come up
with one

morning after —
she asks if I
take sugar

days later
the quarrel
where we left it

kites in the wind
staying together
for the children

Super Bowl Sunday
she asks if there's anything
on television

my side of the quarrel

her eyes on the wall clock

twilight
after her long silence
her long sigh

breaking up . . .
the stuff that belongs
to both of us

winter solitude
the exact shape
of the moon

singles bar
she tells him she always
picks losers

ink

a voice that says
my call is important
cold rain

"no cause for alarm"
says the doctor
causing alarm

NON-UNION
a hardhat eyes
the picketers

CHRIST IS RISEN
on a fast food marquee
southern town

What Heaven
Is Really Like —
nonfiction shelf

winter branch
an itch in a spot
I can't reach

a report on sex
among the elderly
lingering heat

fast food
reading the wall menu
with open mouths

prognosis terminal
his favorite ice cream
melts in the cup

alone again
she tries out a new word —
ex

palmist
reading the lines
in her face

drought
the prayers she knows
by heart

figure skater
the years of practice
in her smile

the years of lying
about her age —
mother's headstone

wind advisory
I cut one more word
from a haiku

prognosis
no more
somedays

winter passes
a few minor revisions
to my death poem

here

my childhood
the dragonfly
knows the way

my home town
the taste
of water

back home where the shortcut used to be

St. Christopher medal —
once I believed
in grownups

the vacant lot
we called a field
my childhood

a girl who looks like
a girl I used to know
my home town

my home town
asking a stranger
for directions

city limits gradually the stars

lawn statues
Jesus outnumbered
by his mother

back home
all the reasons
I left

obituary
my high school sweetheart
who never knew she was

whatever I was doing butterfly

yearbook
whatever became
of me

family album
the stories we tell
the camera

home town
an old love
at last Mass

careful what I wish for one more spring

.

after a visit
to my home town
coming home

day's end . . .
slow dancing
by myself

Acknowledgements

My thanks to the editors of *Acorn, Autumn Moon, Failed Haiku, First Frost, Frogpond, Modern Haiku, Presence, Prune Juice,* and *The Heron's Nest*, in which some of these poems originally appeared, sometimes in a slightly different form.

To my fellow members of Inkstone Poetry and the Spring Street Group,

To all my fellow travelers on the haiku path,

To Jim Kacian, who makes it all happen,

And, once again, to Pat, who makes it all worth while.

Bill Kenney taught for four decades in the English Department of Manhattan College, retiring in 1998. He began writing haiku in 2004. His work has been published in leading haiku journals and has been selected fifteen times for inclusion in the annual *Red Moon Anthology of English Language Haiku*. This is his fourth collection of haiku. His previous collections, *the earth pushes back* (2016), *senior admission* (2018), and *keep walking* (2021) were all published by Red Moon Press. All have been shortlisted for, and the last won, the Touchstone Distinguished Books Award from The Haiku Foundation.